DANIEL G. BRAVO

LUKE 15:

THE FATHER OF THE

DIVINE MERCY

FIRST EDITION

SAN MARCOS'
DE LEÓN

Decree

THOMAS G. WENSKI

by the grace of God and favor of the Apostolic See
Archbishop of Miami

The three books *"Luke 15: The Father of the Divine Mercy, Lucas 15: El Padre de la Divina Misericordia, and Misericordia: Centro del Cristianismo"* have been carefully reviewed and found free of anything which is contrary to the faith or morals as taught by the Roman Catholic Church.

Therefore, in accord with canon 824 of the *Code of Canon Law*, I grant the necessary *approbatio* for the publications of *"Luke 15: The Father of the Divine Mercy, Lucas 15: El Padre de la Divina Misericordia, and Misericordia: Centro del Cristianismo."*

This *imprimatur* is an official declaration that these texts are free of doctrinal or moral error and may be published. No implication is contained therein that the one granting this *imprimatur* agrees with the contents, opinions or statements expressed by the author of the texts.

Given in Miami, Florida, on the 12 of June in the Year of our Lord Two Thousand and Fifteen.

Archbishop of Miami

Attestatio et Nihil Obstat

Cancellarius

Eternal thanks to Jesus, for entering in my heart and for all of the Emmaus brothers that said Yes to the call for service. To my beautiful wife, to my beloved sons Daniel, Diego and Juan Pablo† and my daughter Camila. To my parents for been an example for my family and especially to my Dad, who with his skepticism in the Christian faith, has helped me like he never imagine, for the elaboration of this book.

The Lord is gracious and full of Compassion, Slow to Anger and grate in Mercy.

Psalm 145:8

Thank you Lord, for all this Love and your Mercy.

JESUS CHRIST HAS RISEN!

Daniel G. Bravo.

CONTENTS

Introduction _____ 1

The Public. Luke 15 1-2 _____ 5

The Lost Sheep. Luke 15 3-7 _____ 8

The Lost Coin. Luke 15 8-10 _____ 11

The free will. Luke 15 11-32 _____ 12

The Prodigal Son. Luke 15:13 _____ 14

The Great Famine. Luke 15:14 _____ 15

The Hunger. Luke 15:16 _____ 16

The Estate of the Father. Luke 15:17_____ 17

The Plan. Luke 15:18 _____ 18

The Action. Luke 15, 20a _____ 18

The Compassion. Luke 15: 20b _____ 19

The Forgiveness. Luke 15:20c _____25

The Confession. Luke 15:21 _____ 25

The Restitution. Luke 15:22 _____ 27

The Celebration. Luke 15:23 _____ 28

The Older Brother. Luke 15:25 _____ 29

The Anger. Luke 15:28 _____ 32

The Claim. Luke 15:29 _____ 33

The Father's Response. Luke 15:31 _____ 38

The Inconclusive Ending _____41

Pope Francis March 17, 2013 Angelus ____53

Pope Francis April 8, 2013 Homily _____56

Pope Francis July 5, 2013 Homily _____60

Pope Francis September 15, 2013 Angelus 62

Saint Agustin (S. 112 A, 6-7) Homily _____66

The Divine Mercy _____68

Biography of Saint Faustina Kowalska __81

The Chaplet of the Divine Mercy_____89

INTRODUCTION

This book was made with the main purpose that the person that reads it discover the message of Love that God has for all and each of us.

God loves all of us. We have doubts about His Love because we want to understand with our limited intelligence, God's infinite wisdom.

Jesus gave us a complete Chapter as a gift that teaches us about God's capacity of Love, without caring about the mistakes that could have been committed.

Saint Luke the evangelist, inspired by the Holy Spirit, wrote one of the most important Chapters of the New Testament.

The Chapter is the number 15, also called the Chapter of Mercy. Jesus, using 3 parables, talks to us directly through these parables. He explains to us His capacity to Love and to Forgive.

The richness of this Chapter is huge, infinite. A plethora of men and women have fallen in love with Jesus's message in these parables, including myself. Many books have been written about the parables in this Chapter with a lot of interpretations, but not many have been made about the Chapter as a whole.

In this Chapter we hear about sheep and coins. We hear about two sons and one father, about angels, parties, sacrifices, compassion, forgiveness, etc. Jesus includes all of us in His message, followers and detractors. The messages of these parables defy that audience. Jesus, since His birth, defies every concept. Followers of Him or not, we have to recognize His importance in history, how his message changed the world in a before and an After of Christ.

Even though these parables tell us about sheep, coins and sons, the center of these parables is God's Compassion. The message of Love is transmitted through these parables and they should be read taking into account that God is the main character and the people most precious to Him is Us, His Sons. He compares us with sheep and coins because He wants us to understand his message.

When reading this Chapter and trying to

understand the ways of a Sheppard or the ways of a women or simply the ways of a father, is not correct because in reality, it's Jesus. It is him who compares each moment in the Chapter 15 with Heaven and with God Himself.

To be able to understand the message that God transmits to us through His Word, it is necessary to have Faith that the chapters that we are reading are not simple words for men.

This book is just another about the Chapter of Mercy, and I am just another man that has fallen in love with the message of Love and infinite Mercy. Another man that has witnessed the power that Love and Forgiveness can do to our life.

When we read the Word of God, it's God Himself who is talking. It's through the Holy Spirit that we can receive His message. That is the reason why we are going to use the Word of God to guide us towards receiving His message.

Let's ask God the Faith and Wisdom, so we can understand.

DANIEL G. BRAVO

LUKE 15:
The Father of the Divine Mercy
THE PUBLIC

Luke 15:1-2

"The tax collectors and sinners were all drawing near to listen to him, but the Pharisees and scribes began to complain, saying, 'This man welcomes sinners and eats with them.'"

This Parable starts by placing us in context; The Lord gives these teachings surrounded by followers and detractors, people who loved Him and followed Him and also to the ones that listened just to criticize. From these groups, some listened and understood and others never did. Never the less Jesus didn't judge, He did not hold the message only for the ones that listened to Him. Jesus with His infinite capacity to Love sows the seeds without distinguishing the quality of the soil that receives it.

In the book of Saint Luke Chapter 8, Jesus himself explains to us the reason why He sows the Word to followers and detractors

5

without exception. Been the seed the Word of God.

The Parable of the Sower

Luke 8:4-8

"With a large crowd gathering and people from every town finding their way to him, he told this parable: 'A sower went out to sow his seed. Now as he sowed, some fell on the edge of the path and was trampled on; and the birds of the air ate it up. Some seed fell on rock, and when it came up it withered away, having no moisture. Some seed fell in the middle of thorns and the thorns grew with it and choked it. And some seed fell into good soil and grew and produced its crop a hundredfold.' Saying this he cried, 'Anyone who has ears for listening should listen!'"

The purpose of the Parables

Lucas 8:9-10

"His disciples asked him what this parable might mean, and he said, 'To you is granted to understand the secrets of the kingdom of God; for the rest it remains in parables, so that they may look but not perceive, listen but not understand."

The Parable of the Sower explained

Lucas 8:11-15

"'This, then, is what the parable means: the seed is the word of God. Those on the edge of the path are people who have heard it, and then the devil comes and carries away the word from their hearts in case they should believe and be saved. Those on the rock are people who, when they first hear it, welcome the word with joy. But these have no root; they believe for a while, and in time of trial they give up. As for the part that fell into thorns, this is people who have heard, but as they go on their way they are choked by the worries and riches and pleasures of life and never produce any crops. As for the part in the rich soil, this is people with a noble and generous heart who have heard the word and take it to themselves and yield a harvest through their perseverance."

After Jesus places us in this context and made us part of the public, He began to teach the Merciful Parables.

Jesus's message is not an easy one, and that

audience wanted to hear that message. Everybody, sinners, publicans, scribes and Pharisees, some wanted to hear because they liked the message that brought them closer to God, but to the others, the message bothered them, that is why they criticized Him. Not only because of the message, but also because of the nature of the other half of the audience that was present.

We should try to visualize this public; every single line in these parables was heard by them. Jesus himself makes sure that we are aware of that fact. Let's try to visualize the audience, some mesmerized by his words and the others criticizing the message and angered about the presence of the others.

Let's enjoy Jesus message to His audience:

THE LOST SHEEP

Luke 15:3-7

So he told them this parable: 'Which one of you with a hundred sheep, if he lost one, would fail to leave the ninety-nine in the desert and go after the missing one till he found it? And when he found it, would he not joyfully take it on his shoulders and

then, when he got home, call together his friends and neighbors, saying to them, **"Rejoice with me**, I have found my sheep that **was lost**." In the same way, I tell you, there will be more **rejoicing in heaven over one sinner repenting** than over ninety-nine upright people who have no need of repentance."

Jesus is talking about Sheep, yes, but He is also talking about you and me, is talking about us, to all of us that have been lost at least once.

If we really pay attention, Jesus explains at the end, what this message really is about.

Lucas 15:7 "I tell you, there will be more rejoicing in heaven over one sinner repenting than over ninety-nine upright people who have no need of repentance."

Sinner = Lost Sheep

Jesus = Sheppard

Jesus, the Good Sheppard Himself, is telling us that there is a REJOICE IN HEAVEN, or a Party in Heaven when a sinner repents.

Hundreds of years before the Word became flesh, the prophet Ezekiel wrote about the Good Sheppard in Chapter 34 of his book.

Ezekiel 34:11-12

"For the Lord Yahweh says this: Look, I myself shall take care of my flock and look after it. As a shepherd looks after his flock when he is with his scattered sheep, so shall I look after my sheep? I shall rescue them from wherever they **have been scattered on the day of clouds and darkness."**

Ezekiel 34:15-16

"I myself shall pasture my sheep, I myself shall give them rest -- declares

the Lord Yahweh. I shall look for the lost one**, bring back the stray, bandage the injured and make the sick strong. I shall watch over the fat and healthy. I shall be a true shepherd to them."**

Jesus continues with his teachings:

THE LOST COIN

Luke 15 8-10

'Or again, what woman with ten drachmas would not, if she lost one, light a lamp and sweep out the house and search thoroughly till she found it? And then, when she had found it, call together her friends and neighbors, saying to them, "Rejoice with me, I have found the drachma I lost." In the same way, I tell you, there is rejoicing among the angels of God over one repentant sinner.'"

Jesus is comparing us once more but, this time he is doing it with something very precious to us. He is compares us with a lost coin that we search until it is found. This coin is so precious that when it is found, we will invite friends and neighbors to celebrate.

The Lord did the same thing He did in the Good Sheppard Parable, but this time He talks about a coin, a lost Drachma, and the attitude of the woman to find it. We have to see between the lines and realize it is also about you and me, about us, God is always searching for us and He Rejoices when we come back to Him.

Luke 15:10

"In the same way, I tell you, there is rejoicing among the angels of God over one repentant sinner.'"

Jesus tells us again that there is REJOICING IN HEAVEN, GOD AND THE ANGELS are rejoicing for a sinner that repent his sins.

Jesus uses the examples of happiness that we feel when we find the Lost Coin for us to have an analogy on the feeling of joy that God has when we come back to Him.

After these two preparing parables, Jesus decides to tell us about the Prodigal Son:

THE FREE WILL

Luke 15 11-12

Then he said, 'There was a man who had two sons.

The younger one said to his father, "Father, let me have the share of the estate that will come to me." So the father divided

the property between them."

Jesus tells us a parable that has 3 characters: A Father, an Older and younger son.

He also tells us that the younger son asks for his share of the estate up front. I imagine it has to be very hard as a Father to have a son that is so desperate for money that it makes you divide the estate while you are still alive.

But this Father agrees to the petition of this younger son and gives him the portion that corresponds to him. In this act, God explains the Free will.

In this parable the Father is not other than God himself and the younger son is you and me. Yes, this is a story of 2 sons and 1 father, but as the parable continues, we will realize that this Father is not a regular Father. We need to remember that before this parable we read two others were God/Father is the Sheppard, God/Father is the Woman, and in this Parable God /Father is The Father.

Our Father doesn't want slaves, He wants His sons and daughters to be free. We have complete freedom even knowing that this freedom can take us to commit mistakes......

That shows how great and respectful is God's Love toward us.

THE PRODIGAL SON

Luke 15:13

"A few days later, the younger collected all his belongings and set off to a distant country where he squandered his inheritance on a life of dissipation."

This younger son not only causes the pain of dividing the estate of the father, asking for his part of his will in advance, but worse than that. He goes on to sell his part of the estate and leaves the house of his father to live in a faraway country.

This younger son squanders all his inheritance, loses all his estate on that far away country. This irresponsible action is what gives him the name Prodigal Son. Prodigal means: a person who spends money in a recklessly extravagant way.

This is the sole reason of how this younger son, becomes the Prodigal Son.

THE GREATE FAMINE

Luke 15:14

"'When he had spent it all, that country experienced a severe famine, and now he began to feel the pinch; so he hired himself out to one of the local inhabitants who put him on his farm to feed the pigs."

This son had everything in the house of his father, but he then loses everything including his dignity. His disgrace is so great and was in such a need that he started to take care of pigs. Pigs are animals that were forbidden for the Jewish people at the time of Jesus. This man has fallen so low because of his wrongful actions that he forced himself to take care of pigs, an impure animal. Not only that, from having a fortune, the Prodigal Son now is forced to work as a servant to a non-Jewish man. I ask myself, can Jesus give any example in this parable to show how low this man has fallen? One thing is sure, every Jewish present while Jesus was telling the parable knew how bad and low this son fell.

It is important to remember the audience while Jesus told the parables:

Luke 15:1-2

"The tax collectors and sinners were all drawing near to listen to him, but the Pharisees and scribes began to complain, saying, 'This man welcomes sinners and eats with them.'"

The Pharisees were Jewish that belonged to a Judaism faction. The Scribes were scholars in the Word of God, on the Torah. These groups, most certainly, were above in "knowledge about God" than the rest of the people that were listening to the parables and maybe they identified each and all the mistakes, faults, sins that the Prodigal Son made.

THE HUNGER

Luke 15:16

"And he would willingly have filled himself with the husks the pigs were eating but no one would let him have them."

This son, can't fall any lower. His hunger is so great that he wanted to feed himself with the food of the pigs. Now let's remember how dirty pigs are, how unsanitary the food of the pigs truly is. Food that is composed of the mud created by their own discharges.... How bad has to be your hunger that you are even considering to feed from that. This man envied the animals that he considered impure, and the most horrible fact was, he was not allowed to eat the pigs food. He was living real hell.

Jesus is showing us, is telling us, how low we can fall when we distance ourselves from God and his Love. When we give more value to the World than his Word, when we go after material things instead of his Love. When convinced by our "own capacities", we become doers of our free will and we take the wrong path.

THE ESTATE OF THE FATHER

Lucas 15:17

"Coming to his senses he thought, "How many of my father's hired workers have more than enough food to eat, but here am I, dying from hunger"."

In his desperation, he remembers, in a very conscious way, about the great mistake that he has made by leaving all that he had. He is ruined, desperate, starving to death, just for leaving the house of his Father.

THE PLAN

Lucas 15:18-19

"I shall get up and go to my father and I shall say to him: "Father, I have sinned against heaven and against you; I no longer deserve to be called your son; treat me as one of your hired men.""

He plans what he is going to do and what he is going to say. How many times have we planned to change or to do something that we never do? We know how different it is to plan and to execute the plan. Between planning and taking action there are a lot of differences.

THE ACTION

Luke 15, 20 a

"So he got up and went back to his father."

To make plans is simple, a plan to change something that is not right is simple, but to change, really change from the heart, is only possible with the grace of God, a gift of God and the Love of God.

He got up = he arose = in Koine Greek (original language of the book of Saint Luke) the word used was Anistemi.

This action to Rise Up was without of doubt an act by the Grace of God. We know this because the Verb chosen by Saint Luke was Anistemi, and this Verb has a special meaning. Anistemi doesn't just mean the simple action of standing up, no. Anistemi has a bigger meaning, has another connotation. It goes beyond any regular act of rising. Anistemi implies a change of life, only given by the Grace of God as a Gift.

God himself gives us this gift of having the strength to make this decision. The very decision that takes us home. God is always present in an Action that comes with Good outcome and isn't present when Actions are made for Bad things.

THE COMPASSION

Luke 15: 20b

"While he was still a long way off, his father saw him and was moved with compassion. "

This Loving Father was waiting the return of

his son, and when He saw him, He felt COMPASSION. He forgave his son because of his COMPASSION. That COMPASSION led Him to forgive. That COMPASSION together with the act of forgiveness converts to Mercy.

The Word COMPASSION in Koine Greek is ESPLANCHNISTHE. This word is the one that the Holy Spirit inspired Saint Luke to write in the Gospel where these parables are located. The word means to have Compassion for a person with a feeling that comes from the entrails, from the guts, to have pity, to have Mercy, to be moved with compassion. **STRONGS NT 4697: σπλαγχνίζομαι**

We know the Gospels were written in Koine Greek, Saint Luke inspired, chose the word ESPLANCHNISTHE (σπλαγχνίζομαι). Later on, Saint Luke's Gospel was translated to Latin and the words chosen to replace ESPLANCHNISTHE were: **misericordia motus est** means (Moved with Compassion).

The majority of translations from Latin to English, translates the Word ESPLANCHNISTHE (σπλαγχνίζομαι):

moved with Compassion.

St. Thomas Aquinas defined the virtue of "mercy" in his Summa Theologiae as "the compassion in our hearts for another person's misery, a compassion which drives us to do what we can to help him" (ST II-II.30.1). For St. Thomas, this virtue has two aspects: "affective" mercy and "effective" mercy.

Affective mercy is an emotion: the pity we feel for the plight of another. In this respect, St. Thomas says, human mercy is grounded in a "defect" in our nature: the defect of human vulnerability to suffering. We feel pity for those who suffer because we, too, are subject to such miseries. Thus, our affective sympathy for others arises from our capacity for empathy. Saint Thomas notes: "Those who reckon themselves happy and so powerful that no ill may befall them are not so compassionate" (II-II.30.2). To some extent, however, the intensity of our affective mercy for the plight of another also depends upon how closely we are united to others in friendship: "The person who loves regards his friend as another self, and so he counts his friend's troubles as his own, and grieves over them as if they were his own" (II-II.30.2). An affective bond, we might say, easily forms between friends, and this renders good friends all the more capable of sympathy for each other's plight. For example, when we hear that a friend or a loved one is about to go through a major surgery, we naturally feel compassion for them, and we say to ourselves, "I can imagine what anxiety my friend is going through right now on the eve of his operation." We can "imagine" it because we have been sick and in need of medical treatment ourselves. This sympathetic empathy is what St. Thomas means by "affective mercy."

Effective mercy, on the other hand, is something that we do, a positive action for the good of another, taking steps to relieve the miseries or meet the needs of others. According to St. Thomas, the Latin word misericordia literally means "having a miserable heart" — both affectively and effectively — for another person's misery.

To have Mercy is to take action moved from the inside with Compassion.

That Mercy comes from the LOVE that GOD has for you, for me, for us.

Chapter 15 is called the Chapter of Mercy, and this part of the parable is the reason for that.

This Merciful Father is God himself. Let's remember, in the first two parables the Sheppard is God searching and finding his lost Sheep that is the sinner. The woman is also God, not resting until she finds her lost coin. At the end of the parable we know that the coin is us the sinners and that God never stopped looking for us and to rejoice and celebrate after the finding. The father is God himself, who not once stopped looking over the horizon waiting for his lost son,

the prodigal one, the one that never valued the relationship with his Father/God.

The Catechesis of the Catholic Church in the numeral 2447 defines the Works of Mercy:

CORPORAL WORKS OF MERCY

- Feed the hungry.
- Give drink to the thirsty.
- Clothe the naked.
- Help those imprisoned.
- Shelter the homeless.
- Visit the sick.
- Bury the dead.

SPIRITUAL WORKS OF MERCY

- Admonish the sinner (Give correction to those who need it).

- Instruct the ignorant (Share our knowledge with others).

- Counsel the doubtful (Give advice to those who need it).

- Comfort the sorrowful (Comfort those who suffer).

- Bear wrongs patiently (Be patient with others).

- Forgive all injuries (Forgive those who hurt us).

- Pray for the living and the dead.

We the Christians only think about Mercy when God forgives us or helps us when we are in need but we forget that Mercy is what Jesus wants us to have. If Jesus asks us to have Mercy, it is because he can help us to feel the Compassion that comes from the inside and we are called to transform that feeling into actions such as: Feeding the hungry, Giving drinks to the thirsty, Clothe the naked. Help those imprisoned, Shelter the homeless, Visit the sick, and bury the dead.

THE FORGIVENESS

Luke 15:20c

"He ran to his son, clasped him in his arms and kissed him."This Compassionate, Merciful Father was moved with the great Love He had for his son, that as soon as He saw him he RAN!

It's incredible to see how a powerful man, with servants, an estate, etc., that was dishonored by his son; that decided to leave his father for money, has the capacity to have Compassion and take that into the action of Forgiveness, moved by unconditional Love. This Father is not a regular Father, this Father is GOD.

THE CONFESSION

Luke 15:21

"Then his son said, "Father, I have sinned against heaven and against you. I no longer deserve to be called your son.""

The son received kisses and hugs, but still talks to his Father, confessing with words, his sin.

We consider this act of communicating the sins as the act of confession. It's important to bring to actual words the things that we have done wrong. That is the reason why, Jesus giving us this parable, shows us an example and the how to do it. **"Father, I have sinned against heaven and against you. I no longer deserve to be called your son."** This should be the beginning of all confessions.

Psalm 32:5-6

"I made my sin known to you, did not conceal my guilt. I said, 'I shall confess my offence to Yahweh.' And you, for your part, took away my guilt, forgave my sin. That is why each of your faithful ones prays to you in time of distress. Even if great floods overflow, they will never reach your faithful."

It's our duty to ask for forgiveness and to do it with spoken words, not only with thoughts. One thing is to plan and another is to take the thoughts and convert them into the act of asking for forgiveness. When forgiveness is spoken with real words, it brings with it action, something more powerful than the simple thought. The return to Home is not complete until that verbal confession is made, in a clear, sincere, and real tone with the purpose of amendment. It's especially about that, the purpose of amendment, to ask for forgiveness. Without the purpose of amendment, we are lying to ourselves and even worse, lying to our Father that loves us. Without purpose of amendment, we are returning to that far away country, we will neither be happy nor complete, and we will become prodigal sons again. When we don't amend our mistakes, aren't we wasting our Love relationship with God?

THE RESTITUTION

Luke 15:22

"But the father said to his servants, "Quick! Bring out the best robe and put it on him; put a ring on his finger and sandals on his feet."

The best robe means the best clothes, the Ring, the sandals; this Father forgives this son that sins against Him and repents. He restores all the rights of his son without conditions. The restoration is complete.

THE CELEBRATION

Luke 15:23

"Bring the calf we have been fattening, and slaughter it; we will celebrate by having a feast, because this son of mine was dead and has come back to life; he was lost, and has been found." And they began to celebrate."

The Rejoice of the Father is so great, that he offers to sacrifice the best calf. This is a thanksgiving sacrifice; once again, it's important to remember the audience that was present, the Pharisees and the Scribes. They should have been offended listening to Jesus talk about a Merciful Father that forgives his son that committed terrible sins. The same thing happened with the Lost Sheep and the missing Coin. Remember after the find/return, there is always CELEBRATION IN HEAVEN. God uses the term lost and found, but if we think about it, the prodigal son was

lost by his own mistakes, his own sins, and returned because he recognized it. He plans his return and with the Grace of God, he actually returns, and the Father from the Parable says: **"we will celebrate by having a feast, because this son of mine was dead and has come back to life; he was lost, and has been found."**

THE OLDER BROTHER

Luke 15:25-27

"'Now the elder son was out in the fields, and on his way back, as he drew near the house, he could hear music and dancing. Calling one of the servants he asked what it was all about. The servant told him, "Your brother has come, and your father has killed the calf we had been fattening because he has got him back safe and sound."'"

At this moment of the parable enters a character. Jesus is clear at the beginning saying that there were 2 sons, a Young one and an older one. This older brother was not mentioned in the parable until this moment.

Where was this older brother when his brother asked his father the part of his living will?

Jesus presents a complete absence of this

brother until now.

It is very important once again, to remember the audience, the two groups present when Jesus was giving us these parables.

The first group: The "publicans and sinners." This group represents the non-Jewish (the Publicans) and the sinners (Jewish and not Jewish), that's why, this first group is represented in the parable as the Prodigal Son or younger brother. God loving us all in the same way and expecting us to be Saints, both, publicans and sinners, are sons of the Father that chose to be far from Him, by their own choice.

The second group: The "Pharisees and the Scribes of the Law". This group represents the ones that follow the law, the faithful followers of the teachings of the God of Abraham, the ones that are always with the their Father, the guardians of the Law. Educated in the scriptures, the Torah, the Psalms, etc. This second group is represented in the parable as the Older brother or Older son. God loving us all in the same way and wanting us Saints. Both, Pharisees and

Scribes, are sons of the Father that chose to be far from Him, by their own choice

Jesus with his infinite wisdom presents to us these two brothers and He puts us also in perspective, today 2000 year later, that there are still two groups: The "Far Away ones" and the "Closer ones".

In the Parable we have heard already how the group of the "Far Away ones", represented by the Younger son (also called the Prodigal son) made the decision (enlighten by the Holy Spirit) to return to the House of the Father, who filled with the Compassion that comes from the insides, Forgave his son immediately.

In the part of the Parable that follows, we are going to hear Jesus talking to the second group, the "Closer ones".

Let us continue with the reading, to understand Jesus's message to us.

THE ANGER

Luke 15:28

"He was angry then and refused to go in, and his father came out and began to urge him to come in;"

The Older brother filled with Angry, doesn't want to participate in the rejoicing of his Father.

It is necessary for us to understand that Jesus has been placing us in context, has been telling us that the Sheppard is God and that we are the Sheep. The same with the coin and the woman. Let's remember that this is not about a human Father, this is about God the Father.

Let's not read this Parable trying to understand Jesus's teachings with human laws and human attitudes. Instead let's try to understand that it's God himself the one that is giving us the message of Love and Salvation.

THE CLAIM

Luke 15:29-30

"but he retorted to his father, "All these years I have slaved for you and never once disobeyed any orders of yours, yet you never offered me so much as a kid for me to celebrate with my friends. But, for this son of yours, when he comes back after swallowing up your property -- he and his loose women -- you kill the calf we had been fattening.""

The Older Brother tries to explain to his Father the reason why he was mad. He brings up the past to make the father understand. Let's remember that the Older Brother is represented by the second group, the group at the time of Jesus when He was giving this Parable. The Jewish people had a serving relationship with God that was already more than 3000 year old. This second group, the Pharisees and the Scribes, were the ones that complain to Jesus because **'This man welcomes sinners and eats with them.'** This complain is about Jesus and his relationship with the first Group.

The Complain of the Older Son to the Father goes beyond. If we analyze the Parable, we will notice that there was no relationship between the brothers, neither after the departure of the younger one, nor while the younger one was in the far away country, nor at the return. Jesus doesn't mention any interaction that can tell us that there is a relationship between them. Then, how could his Older Brother know all the things that his Younger brother did in that Far Away Country?

We can deduct that the Older Brother filled his thought with imagination while his brother was abroad. Maybe that Older Brother knew the weaknesses of his younger Son and simply deducted what he did in that far away country.

We can only rely on the facts and these facts are that the Older brother didn't know for sure what his younger brother did and all his critic was based on mere conjecture, wild guesses, pure imagination.

There is also a claim, not only he (the older brother) makes a false testimony not proved against his younger brother. He also has the audacity to make a claim to his Father. We know from the last two parables that Jesus was telling us that the Father was God himself.

This is not a regular Father, this Father is God. Who are we to throw a claim to God?

This second group represented by the older brother, is making a false testimony against the first group.

This Scribes and Pharisees are criticizing God's decisions, as a matter of fact; they were doing that since the beginning of the Chapter:

Luke 15:2 "but the Pharisees and scribes began to complain, saying, 'This man welcomes sinners and eats with them.'"

The arrogance of this group is taking them to make a big mistake, been the ones that knew the Word of God, they perfectly well knew the 10 commandments, been the first three about Loving God above all things.

Saint Luke tells us in the Chapter 10, after the parable of the Good Samaritan, how good was the knowledge that the Scribes and

Pharisees had on the Word of God and His Laws: **Luke 10:25 "And now a lawyer stood up and, to test him, asked, 'Master, what must I do to inherit eternal life?'He said to him, 'What is written in the Law? What is your reading of it?'He replied, 'You must love the Lord your God with all your heart, with all your soul, with all your strength, and with all your mind, and your neighbor as yourself.' Jesus said to him, 'You have answered right, do this and life is yours.'"**

This Older Brother knew that he should love God, His Father, above all things and that he should love his neighbor like himself. This includes of course, love his younger brother, like himself.

Ever more, in the Parable of the Good Samaritan, Jesus goes beyond. He asks us to have compassion, the same compassion that He had, that the Father had, with the Prodigal Son. Jesus wants from us to behave like the Samaritan, He want us to behave like Him, like the Father of the Parable, like God himself.

Luke 10:31-37

"Now a priest happened to be travelling

down the same road, but when he saw the man, he passed by on the other side. In the same way a Levite who came to the place saw him, and passed by on the other side.

But a Samaritan traveler who came on him was moved with compassion when he saw him.He went up to him and bandaged his wounds, pouring oil and wine on them. He then lifted him onto his own mount and took him to an inn and looked after him.

Next day, he took out two denarius and handed them to the innkeeper and said, "Look after him, and on my way back I will make good any extra expense you have."

Which of these three, do you think, proved himself a neighbor to the man who fell into the bandits' hands?'

He replied, 'The one who showed pity towards him.' Jesus said to him, 'Go, and do the same yourself.'"

Was the Older Brother behaving like the Good Samaritan?

Where is his Compassion?

This brother has lived all these years with his

father and has not learned the most important lesson. He doesn't know his Father, doesn't know the real message of God. They have eyes but don't see; they have ears but don't hear.

I ask myself, what is a worse sin? Get away from God, because of the Sin, recognize the mistake and come back to Him or knowing exactly what God wants, criticize Him and even worse, create a false testimony about your neighbor in this case, your own younger brother?

Only God is the Judge, it's not for us to determine which of the sins is the worst, but something is clear, both groups are sinners.

THE FATHER'S RESPONSE

Luke 15:31-32

"'The father said, "My son, you are with me always and all I have is yours.

But it was only right we should celebrate and rejoice, because your brother here was dead and has come to life; he was lost and is found."'"

Here God shows us again His infinite Love.

Knowing what is in the heart of the older brother, he also forgives him. This Merciful Father tells this son that criticizes Him that all He has is his. He says that in present tense, even more; this Father invites his older son to celebrate.

This Father doesn't distinguish, only Loves us, it is us the ones that chose to leave from his presence.

This older brother with his attitude, is leaving the house of his father, just like his younger brother did but for a different reason. He fails his father and by doing so, creates a distance between them.

This Merciful Father, is pure Love, with infinite Love for us.

The invitation for the older brother is to rejoice with Him and to Celebrate.

Jesus uses the same words that He used in all the parables of the Chapter 15. By doing that, He is letting us know that it is the same the message all the time. **Luke 15:32 "But it was only right we should celebrate and rejoice, because your brother here was** dead and has come to life; he was lost and is found."Luke 15:7 In the same way, I tell you, there will be more **rejoicing** in heaven over one sinner repenting than over ninety-nine upright people who have no need of repentance. Luke 15:9-10 And then, when she had found it, call together her friends and neighbors, saying to them, **"Rejoice with me**, I have found the drachma I lost." In the same way, I tell you, there is **rejoicing among the angels of God** over one repentant sinner.'

The parallelism between the parables is Key. Jesus' message is clear when we are placed in context and when we read the Chapter of Mercy complete.

Both sons received the forgiveness of the Father; both were invited to celebrate and to be the heirs of His kingdom.

The parable of the Prodigal Son and the Chapter of Mercy, end like this, with an invitation to celebrate and to rejoice.

THE INCONCLUSIVE ENDING

We will never know if that older brother from the parable, entered the celebration, or not?

Knowing that the older brother represents the second group of the ones present while Jesus told the parables of Mercy, we can have an idea to what could have been the end.

Jesus leaves an opened end for this parable; He doesn't tell us what happened between the Father and his Older Son.

Did these groups of Pharisees and Scribes understand the message of Mercy that Jesus gave to them through the whole Chapter?

believe that they did not understand, why? If this second group of listeners would have understood the message, Jesus would never have suffered a death on the Cross. Jesus would never have been given up by His own people. The Pharisees and Scribes were very educated in their faith; Jesus had the same level of knowledge (infinite more of course). It is very well documented that the 3 years that His Gospels lasted, Jesus behaved like a faithful Jew, a close follower of the rites of

His people, He participated in all of the Jewish celebrations.

The Pope Benedict XVI in his book: Jesus of Nazareth form the Baptism to the Transfiguration, explains to us, this key part of the Reading.

The parable breaks off here; it tells us nothing about the older brother's reaction. Nor can it, because at this point the parable immediately passes over into reality. Jesus is using these words of the father to speak to the heart of the murmuring Pharisees and scribes who have grown indignant at his goodness to sinners (cf Lk 15:2). It now becomes fully clear that Jesus identifies his goodness to sinners with the goodness of the father in the parable and that all the words attributed to the father are the words that he himself addresses to the righteous. The parable does not tell the story of some distant affair, but is about what is happening here and now . through him. He is wooing the heart of his adversaries. He begs them to come in and to share his joy at this hour of homecoming and reconciliation. These words remain in the Gospel as a pleading invitation. Paul takes up this pleading invitation when he writes: "We beseech you on behalf of Christ, be reconciled to God" (2

Cor 5:20).

On one hand, then, the parable is located quite realistically at the moment in history when Christ recounted it. At the same time, however, it points beyond the historical moment, for God's wooing and pleading continues. But to whom is the parable now addressed? The Church Fathers generally applied the two brothers motif to the relation between Jews and Gentiles. It was not hard for them to recognize in the dissolute son who had strayed far from God and from himself an image of the pagan world, to which Jesus had now opened the door for communion with God in grace and for which he now celebrates the feast of his love. By the same token. neither was it hard for them to recognize in the brother who remained at home an image of the people of Israel, who could legitimately say: "Lord, these many years I have served you, and I never disobeyed one of your commands." Israel's fidelity and image of God are clearly revealed in such fidelity to the Torah.

This application to the Jews is not illegitimate so long as we respect the form in which we have found it in the text: as God's delicate attempt to talk Israel round, which remains entirely God's initiative. We should note that the father in the parable not only does not dispute the older brother's fidelity, but explicitly confirms his sonship: "My child, you are always with me, and everything that is mine is yours." It would be a false interpretation to read this as a condemnation of the Jews, for which there is no support in the text.

While we may regard this application of the Parable of the Two Brothers to Israel and the Gentiles as one dimension of the text, there are other dimensions as well. After all, what Jesus says about the older brother is aimed not simply at Israel (the sinners who came to him were Jews, too), but at the specific temptation of the righteous, of those who are en regle, at rights with God, as Grelot puts it. In this

connection, Grelot places emphasis on the sentence: "I never disobeyed one of your commandments." For them, more than anything else God is Law; they see themselves in a juridical relationship with God and in that relationship they are at rights with him. But God is greater: They need to convert from the Law-God to the greater God, the God of love. This will not mean giving up their obedience, but rather that this obedience will flow from deeper wellsprings and will therefore be bigger, more open, and purer, but above all more humble.

Jesus is apprehended the night of Holy Thursday, just four days after his triumph entrance to Jerusalem and from being received like the long waited Messiah to celebrate the Jewish Passover that remembers the Exodus from Egypt. That Thursday after the sun set, Jesus celebrated the Passover Diner, one day earlier than the rest and transformed the celebration forever. That same day, between sun set and sun set, Jesus was delivered, jailed, tortured, spitted, was judged, and taken to the Calvary where He was crucified.

Jesus was so Jewish that He did everything according to the traditions of His people. He passed away at 3pm; at the same time that the Sacrificial Lamb was sacrificed for the Jewish Passover, becoming Himself the Sacrificial Lamb.

Which was Jesus sin? To Love us and to ask us to love Him and to Love our Neighbor, just like He did?.

Jesus took that Love for the Neighbor to the next level. With Jesus, God fulfilled what did not let Abraham do to his son Isaac. Just like Isaac was replaced by a Lamb, God redeemed our sins with the sacrifice of his only Son, Jesus, the Lamb of God.

Yes, that second group of the eldest sons with hard heart, didn't want to recognize the Love message that Jesus had.

Jesus resurrected on the third day, and stayed with us until he ascended to heaven on the 40th day. He asked his disciples to go to Jerusalem to celebrate the Jewish feast of the first fruits, also called Pentecost. What the Jewish people celebrate in Pentecost is the first fruits of the exodus from their slavery from Egypt. Those first fruits were the 10 commandments, and the Law that Moses received 50 after they departed from Egypt. It was during the celebration of Pentecost, 50 days after the resurrection of Jesus, that in Jerusalem and according the Divine plan of God, the Holy Spirit arrived. The first fruit of the Sacrifice of Jesus, sealing the new covenant, the new contract, the one that the prophet Jeremiah talks about. **Jeremiah 31:31-34 "'Look, the days are coming, Yahweh declares, when I shall make a new covenant with the House of Israel (and the House of Judah),** but not like the covenant I made with their ancestors the day I took them by the hand to bring them out of Egypt, a covenant which they broke, even though I was their Master, Yahweh declares. No, this is the covenant I shall make with the House of Israel when those days have come, Yahweh declares.

Within them I shall plant my Law, writing it on their hearts. Then I shall be their God and they will be my people.

There will be no further need for everyone to teach neighbor or brother, saying, "Learn to know Yahweh!" No, they will all know me, from the least to the greatest, Yahweh declares, since I shall forgive their guilt and never more call their sin to mind.'"

The Holy Spirit arrived in the form of tongues of fire and placed Himself atop the head of everyone present in the upper room, including the disciples and the Virgin Mary.

The promise of the Holy Spirit

Acts of Apostles 1:3-11

"He had shown himself alive to them after

his Passion by many demonstrations: for forty days he had continued to appear to them and tell them about the kingdom of God.

While at table with them, he had told them not to leave Jerusalem, but to wait there for what the Father had promised. 'It is', he had said, 'what you have heard me speak about:

John baptized with water but, not many days from now, you are going to be baptized with the Holy Spirit.'

Now having met together, they asked him, 'Lord, has the time come for you to restore the kingdom to Israel?'

He replied, 'It is not for you to know times or dates that the Father has decided by his own authority,

but you will receive the power of the Holy Spirit which will come on you, and then you will be my witnesses not only in Jerusalem but throughout Judaea and Samaria, and indeed to earth's remotest end.'

As he said this he was lifted up while they looked on, and a cloud took him from their sight.

They were still staring into the sky as he went, when suddenly two men in white were standing beside them,

and they said, 'Why are you Galileans standing here looking into the sky?
This Jesus who has been taken up from you into heaven will come back in the same way as you have seen him go to heaven.'"

Acts of Apostles 2:1-14

"So from the Mount of Olives, as it is called, they went back to Jerusalem, a short distance away, no more than
a Sabbath walk;

and when they reached the city they went to the upper room where they were staying;
there were Peter and John, James and Andrew, Philip and
Thomas, Bartholomew and
Matthew, James son of Alphaeus and Simon the Zealot, and Jude son of James.

With one heart all these joined constantly in prayer, together with some women, including Mary the mother of Jesus, and with his brothers."

The coming of the Holy Spirit

Acts of Apostles 2:1-4

"When Pentecost day came round, they had all met together,

when suddenly there came from heaven a sound as of a violent wind which filled the entire house in which they were sitting;

And there appeared to them tongues as of fire; these separated and came to rest on the head of each of them."

It's thanks to the Holy Spirit that the Disciples went to preach the good News to Jerusalem. Jerusalem the Holy City, where every Jewish had to go to the special celebrations like the Passover and Pentecost. Jerusalem was full of visitors, and the great majority were Jewish.

The first fruit of the Holy Spirit was the conversion of 3,000 Jews. Older brothers that received the Good News of the Gospels.

The evangelization of the Jewish people

Acts of Apostles 2:37-41

"Hearing this, they were cut to the heart and said to Peter and the other apostles, 'What are we to do, brothers?'

'You must repent,' Peter answered, 'and every one of you must be baptized in the name of Jesus Christ for the forgiveness of your sins, and you will receive the gift of the Holy Spirit.

The promise that was made is for you and your children and for all those who are far away, for all those whom the Lord our God is calling to himself.'

He spoke to them for a long time using many other arguments, and he urged them, 'Save yourselves from this perverse generation.'

They accepted what he said and were baptized. That very day about three thousand were added to their number."

Let's remember that all the disciples were Jewish. This book was not written to judge the people from Israel, by doing that, we will be offending God, who will see us, like older brothers once again.

The most important message from God is to understand that we are all older brothers and younger brothers, by sinning and judging without proofs, by how much we harden our hearts and also by how much we repent from our sins.

We should be neither the older brother, nor Prodigal Son.

God want us to be Saints, there is no doubt about that, but the journey is not easy. It's good to know that our celestial Father knows this and He is always waiting for us if we fail, if we make mistakes and sin. If we repent for those sins, He will be waiting for us with His arms open, full of Love and Compassion.

Let's always do what the Prodigal Son did, let's always make the decision to come back. God himself will give us the strength and valor to RISE UP and come back to His House, to be received with Hugs and Kisses that come from God's insides and translates in Forgiveness.

We are very lucky to be SONS OF THIS MERCIFUL FATHER.

Our Pope Francis, since the beginning of his pontificate, has brought to us the Message of Mercy and Love. That we need to have the valor to come back to the House of the Father and also soften our hardened hearts, especially for the ones that call ourselves member of the Catholic Church.

Let's hear the message of the Merciful Father, directly from Pope Francis:

POPE FRANCIS, MARCH 17, 2013 ANGELUS

Brothers and Sisters, good morning!

After our first meeting last Wednesday, today I can once again address my greeting to you all! And I am glad to do so on a Sunday, on the Lord's Day! This is beautiful and important for us Christians: to meet on Sundays, to greet each other, to speak to each other as we are doing now, in the square. A square which, thanks to the media, has global dimensions.

On this Fifth Sunday of Lent, the Gospel presents to us the episode of the adulterous woman (cf. Jn 8:1-11), whom Jesus saves from being condemned to death. Jesus' attitude is striking: we do not hear words of scorn, we do not hear words of condemnation, but only words of love, of mercy, which are an invitation to conversion. "Neither do I condemn you; go, and do not sin again" (v. 11). Ah! Brothers and Sisters, God's face is the face of a merciful father who is always patient. Have you thought about God's patience, the patience he has with each one of us? That is his mercy. He always has patience, patience with us, he understands us, he waits for us, he does not tire of forgiving us if we are able to return to him with a contrite heart. "Great is God's mercy", says the Psalm.

In the past few days I have been reading a book by a Cardinal — Cardinal Kasper, a clever theologian, a good theologian — on mercy. And that book did me a lot of good, but do not think I am promoting my cardinals' books! Not at all! Yet it has done me so much good, so much good... Cardinal Kasper said that feeling mercy, that this word changes everything. This is the best thing we can feel: it changes the world. A little mercy makes the world less cold and more just. We need to understand properly this mercy of God, this merciful Father who is so patient.... Let us remember the Prophet Isaiah who says that even if our sins were scarlet, God's love would make them white as snow. This mercy is beautiful! I remember, when I had only just become a bishop in the year 1992, the statue of Our Lady of Fatima had just arrived in Buenos Aires and a big Mass was celebrated for the sick. I went to hear confessions at that Mass. And almost at the end of the Mass I stood up, because I had to go and administer a First Confirmation. And an elderly woman approached me, humble, very humble, and over eighty years old. I looked at her, and I said, "Grandmother" — because in our country that is how we

 address the elderly — do you want to make your confession?". "Yes", she said to me. "But if you have not sinned…". And she said to me: "We all have sins…". "But perhaps the Lord does not forgive them". "The Lord forgives all things", she said to me with conviction. "But how do you know, Madam?" "If the Lord did not forgive everything, the world would not exist". I felt an urge to ask her: "Tell me, Madam, did you study at the Gregorian [University]?", because that is the wisdom which the Holy Spirit gives: inner wisdom focused on God's mercy. Let us not forget this word: God never ever tires of forgiving us! "Well, Father what is the problem?" Well, the problem is that we ourselves tire, we do not want to ask, and we grow weary of asking for forgiveness. He never tires of forgiving, but at times we get tired of asking for forgiveness.

Let us never tire, let us never tire! He is the loving Father who always pardons, who has that heart of mercy for us all. And let us too learn to be merciful to everyone. Let us invoke the intercession of Our Lady who held in her arms the Mercy of God made man.

POPE FRANCIS, APRIL 8, 2013 HOMILY

I would like to emphasize one other thing: God's patience has to call forth in us the courage to return to him, however many mistakes and sins there may be in our life. Jesus tells Thomas to put his hand in the wounds of his hands and his feet, and in his side. We too can enter into the wounds of Jesus, we can actually touch him. This happens every time that we receive the sacraments with faith. Saint Bernard, in a fine homily, says: "Through the wounds of Jesus I can suck honey from the rock and oil from the flinty rock (cf. Deut 32:13), I can taste and see the goodness of the Lord" (On the Song of Songs, 61:4). It is there, in the wounds of Jesus, that we are truly secure; there we encounter the boundless love of his heart. Thomas understood this. Saint Bernard goes on to ask: But what can I count on? My own merits? No, "My merit is God's mercy. I am by no means lacking merits as long as he is rich in mercy. If the mercies of the Lord are manifold, I too will abound in merits" (ibid., 5). This is important: the courage to trust in Jesus' mercy, to trust in his patience, to seek refuge always in the wounds of his love. Saint Bernard even states: "So what if my conscience gnaws at me for my many sins? 'Where sin has abounded, there grace has abounded all the more' (Rom 5:20)" (ibid.). Maybe someone among us here is thinking: my sin is so great, I am as far from God as the younger son in the parable, my unbelief is like that of Thomas; I don't have the courage to go back, to believe that God can welcome me and that he is waiting for me, of all people. But God is indeed waiting for you; he asks of you only the courage to go to him.

How many times in my pastoral ministry have I heard it said: "Father, I have many sins"; and I have always pleaded: "Don't be afraid, go to him, he is waiting for you, he will take care of everything". We hear many offers from the world around us; but let us take up God's offer instead: his is a caress of love. For God, we are not numbers, we are important, indeed we are the most important thing to him; even if we are sinners, we are what is closest to his heart.

Adam, after his sin, experiences shame, he feels naked, he senses the weight of what he has done; and yet God does not abandon him: if that moment of sin marks the beginning of his exile from God, there is already a promise of return, a possibility of return. God immediately asks: "Adam, where are you?" He seeks him out. Jesus took on our nakedness, he took upon himself the shame of Adam, the

nakedness of his sin, in order to wash away our sin: by his wounds we have been healed. Remember what Saint Paul says: "What shall I boast of, if not my weakness, my poverty? Precisely in feeling my sinfulness, in looking at my sins, I can see and encounter God's mercy, his love, and go to him to receive forgiveness.

In my own life, I have so often seen God's merciful countenance, his patience; I have also seen so many people find the courage to enter the wounds of Jesus by saying to him: Lord, I am here, accept my poverty, hide my sin in your wounds, wash it away with your blood. And I have always seen that God did just this – he accepted them, consoled them, cleansed them, and loved them.

Dear brothers and sisters, let us be enveloped by the mercy of God; let us trust in his patience, which always gives us more time. Let us find the courage to return to his house, to dwell in his loving wounds, allowing ourselves be loved by him and to encounter his mercy in the sacraments. We will feel his wonderful tenderness, we will feel his embrace, and we too will become more capable of mercy, patience, forgiveness and love.

POPE FRANCIS, JULY 5 2013 HOMILY

Look at the mercy of Jesus; celebrate with him; keep alive the "memory" of the moment in which we have encountered salvation in our lives. This was the threefold invitation given by Pope Francis during his homily. Among the concelebrants was Cardinal Jorge Liberato Urosa Savino, Archbishop of Caracas, whose presence the Pope emphasized at the beginning of the Mass since it was Venezuela's Independence Day.

In his homily Pope Francis reflected on the day's Gospel passage (Mt 9:9-13) in which the Apostle speaks of his own conversion: the tax collector whom Jesus called to be one of the twelve. The message that Jesus wants to give, the Pope said, is one that people have always had trouble understanding: "I desire mercy, not sacrifice". Our God is indeed a God of mercy. You can see it well in the story of Matthew".

Jesus looks at Matthew and awakens "something new" within him, "something that he did not know". The "gaze of Jesus", explained the Holy Father, makes him feel an interior "wonder", and makes him hear "the call of Jesus: follow me". "It only took a moment" to understand that that look had changed his life forever. And it is in this moment that "Matthew says yes, leaves everything and goes with the Lord".

The first moment of the encounter, which consists of "a deep spiritual experience", is followed by a second experience: that of celebration. The Gospel continues with Jesus sitting at table with publicans and sinners; those who "were rejected by society". But for the Pope this "is the contradiction of the celebration of God: the Lord feasts with sinners". Addressing this point Pope Francis referred to Luke's Gospel (15) where it clearly says that there will be more rejoicing in heaven over one sinner who repents than over 99 righteous people who have no need of repentance. This is why celebration is "very important" for the Pope, because the encounter with Jesus and the mercy of God should be celebrated.

But life is not one big party, says Pope Francis. There is a time for celebration, but then there must be "daily work, fuelled by the memory of that first encounter". It

is the memory of mercy and of that celebration that "gives Matthew, and everyone" who has chosen to follow Christ, the strength "to go forward". This, the Pope added, must be remembered forever.

POPE FRANCIS SEPTEMBER 15 2013 ANGELUS

Dear Brothers and Sisters, Good morning!

In the Liturgy today we read chapter 15 of the Gospel of Luke, which contains three parables of mercy: the lost sheep, the lost coin, and then the longest of them, characteristic of St Luke, the parable of the father of two sons, the "prodigal" son and the son who believes he is "righteous", who believes he is saintly. All three of these parables speak of the joy of God. God is joyful. This is interesting: God is joyful! And what is the joy of God? The joy of God is forgiving, the joy of God is forgiving! The joy of a shepherd who finds his little lamb; the joy of a woman who finds her coin; it is the joy of a father welcoming home the son who was lost, who was as though dead and has come back to life, who has come home. Here is the entire Gospel! Here! The whole Gospel, all of Christianity, is here! But make sure that it is not sentiment, it is not being a "do-gooder"! On the contrary, mercy is the true force that can save man and the world from the "cancer" that is sin, moral evil, spiritual evil. Only love fills the void, the negative chasms that evil opens in hearts and in history. Only love can do this, and this is God's joy!

Jesus is all mercy, Jesus is all love: he is God made man. Each of us, each one of us, is that little lost lamb, the coin that was mislaid; each one of us is that son who has squandered his freedom on false idols, illusions of happiness, and has lost everything. But God does not forget us, the Father never abandons us. He is a patient father, always waiting for us! He respects our freedom, but he remains faithful forever. And when we come back to him, he welcomes us like children into his house, for he never ceases, not for one instant, to wait for us with love. And his heart rejoices over every child who returns. He is celebrating because he is joy. God has this joy, when one of us sinners goes to him and asks his forgiveness.

What is the danger? It is that we presume we are righteous and judge others. We also judge God, because we think that he should punish sinners, condemn them to death, instead of forgiving. So 'yes' then we risk staying outside the Father's house! Like the older brother in the parable, who rather than being content that his brother has returned, grows angry with the father who welcomes him and celebrates. If in our heart there is no mercy, no joy of forgiveness, we are not in communion with God, even if we observe all of his precepts, for it is love that saves, not the practice of precepts alone. It is love of God and neighbor that brings fulfilment to all the Commandments. And this is the love of God, his joy: forgiveness. He waits for us always! Maybe someone has some heaviness in his heart: "But, I did this, I did that...". He expects you! He is your father: he waits for you always!

If we live according to the law "an eye for an eye, a tooth for a tooth", we will never escape from the spiral of evil. The evil one is clever, and deludes us into thinking that with our human justice we can save ourselves and save the world! In reality, only the justice of God can save us! And the justice of God is revealed in the Cross: the Cross is the judgement of God on us all and on this world. But how does God judge us? By giving his life for us! Here is the supreme act of justice that defeated the prince of this world once and for all; and this supreme act of justice is the supreme act of mercy. Jesus calls us all to follow this path: "Be merciful, even as your Father is merciful" (Lk 6:36). I now ask of you one thing. In silence, let's all think... everyone think of a person with whom we are annoyed, with whom we are angry, someone we do not like. Let us think of that person and in silence, at this moment, let us pray for this person and let us become merciful with this person.

Let us now invoke the intercession of Mary, Mother of Mercy.

The Parable of the Prodigal Son is so important, that Saint Augustine of Hippo (354-430 AC) wrote Homilies about it. It is interesting that Saint Augustine mentions the Mercy and the Compassion of the Father and also about the Christological meaning of the embrace of the Father to the son that has return, calling Jesus the arm of the Father, the same way that Pope Benedict XVI did.

Homily of Saint Augustine (Sermon 112 A, 6-7)

"Even though he was still preparing to talk with his father, saying to himself: *I will arise and say to him,* (Lk. 15: 18), the father, knowing his thought from afar, went to meet him. What does *going to meet him* mean, but coming first with his mercy? He says: *Still being far, his father left to meet him moved by mercy.* (Ib. 15:20) Why was he moved by mercy? Because the son had already admitted his misery. *And running towards him, he pressed on him,* that is, he put his arm around the neck of his son. The arm of the Father is the Son; therefore, he gave the prodigal son Christ to carry, a load, that does not weigh him down, but gives relief . . .

The father orders that first he would be given a robe, which Adam had lost upon sinning.

By having received in peace the son and having kissed him, he commands that the son may be given clothing: the hope of immortality that baptism confers. He orders as well that he may be given a ring, the pledge of the Holy Spirit, and shoes for his feet as preparation for the Gospel of peace, so that the feet of the one who proclaims may be beautiful. God does all these through his servants, that is, through the ministers of the Church. Then, do the ministers give clothing, ring and shoes from their own? They fulfill their ministry, they give themselves to their office, but the one who grants is that One from whose storeroom and treasure these things are taken. He also gave instruction to kill the fatted calf, that is, he admitted the prodigal son to his table at which Christ, who was slain, is served as nourishment. For all who come to the Church from a distant region, the fatted calf is killed, when the death of Christ is preached, and he is then admitted to take part of his body. The fatted calf is killed, because he, who had been lost, has been found."

The Mercy of God has no limits. God wants us to embrace his Mercy so much, that at the beginning of the XX Century, chose to send His Divine Mercy message to a woman called Elena Kowalska. We know her as Saint Faustina Kowalska, who by the mandate of Jesus had to give us His Mercy and has to see us receive the message of Jesus himself.

God's Mercy never changes, it's always the same, it's a Compassion that comes from his entrails. It's the same Mercy that He has for us and that asks us to have for our neighbors. That is also the center of Saint Faustina's Diary. Here are some fragments about God's Compassion.

THE DIVINE MERCY

Saint Faustina Kowalska (1905-1938) canonized by the Pope John Paul II in April 30th of 2000.

The Divine Mercy:

O Incomprehensible God, how great is Your mercy! It surpasses the combined understanding of all men and angels. All the angels and all humans have emerged from the **very depths of Your tender mercy**.

Mercy is the flower of love. God is love, and mercy is His deed. In love it is conceived; in mercy it is revealed. Everything I look at speaks to me of God's mercy. Even God's very justice speaks to me about His fathomless mercy, because justice flows from love. (Diary 651)

Write this: Everything that exists is enclosed **in the bowels of My mercy,** more deeply than an infant in its mother's womb. How painfully distrust of My goodness wounds Me! Sins of distrust wound Me most painfully. **(Diary 1076)**

God, You did not destroy man after his fall, but in Your mercy You forgave him, You forgave in a divine way; that is, not only have You absolved him from guilt, but You have bestowed upon him every grace. Mercy has moved You to deign to descend among us and lift us up from our misery. God will descend to earth; the Immortal Lord of lords will abase Himself. But where will You descend, Lord; will it be to the temple of Solomon? Or will You have a new tabernacle built for Yourself? Where do You intend to come down? O Lord, what kind of tabernacle shall we prepare for You, since the whole earth is Your footstool?

You have indeed prepared a tabernacle for Yourself: the Blessed Virgin. Her Immaculate Womb is Your dwelling place, and the inconceivable miracle of Your mercy takes place, O Lord. The Word becomes flesh; God dwells among us, the Word of God, Mercy Incarnate. By Your descent, You have lifted us up to Your divinity. Such is the excess of Your love, the abyss of Your mercy. Heaven is amazed at the superabundance of Your love. No one fears to approach You now. You are the God of mercy. **You have compassion on misery**. You are our God, and we are your people. You are our Father, and we are Your children by grace.

Praise be to Your mercy, that You have deigned to descend among us. (Diary 1745)

Today, in the course of a long conversation, the Lord said to me, How very much I desire the salvation of souls! My dearest secretary, write that I want to pour out My divine life into human souls and sanctify them, if only they were willing to accept My grace. The greatest sinners would achieve great sanctity, if only they would trust in My mercy. **The very inner depths of My being are filled to overflowing with mercy,** and it is being poured out upon all I have created (Diary 1784)

Jesus stood before me and said, **Look into My Heart and see there the love and mercy which I have for humankind, and especially for sinners. Look, and enter into My Passion.** (Diary 1663)

Oh, if sinners knew My mercy, they would not perish in such great numbers. Tell sinful souls not to be afraid to approach Me; speak to them of My great mercy." (Diary,1396)

I am Thrice Holy, and detest the smallest sin. I cannot love a soul which is stained with sin; but when it repents, there is no limit to My generosity toward it. My mercy embraces and justifies it. With My mercy, I pursue sinners along all their paths, and My Heart rejoices when they return to Me. I forget the bitterness with which they fed My Heart and rejoice at their return. (Diary,1728)

My daughter, write that the greater the misery of a soul, the greater it's right to My mercy; [urge] all souls to trust in the unfathomable abyss of My mercy, because I want to save them all. On the cross, the fountain of My mercy was opened wide by the lance for all souls – no one have I excluded! (Diary,1182)

My Secretary, write that I am more generous toward sinners that toward the just. It was for their sake that I came down from heaven; it was for their sake that My Blood was spilled. Let them not fear to approach Me; they are most in need of My mercy. (Diary,1275)

I desire that priests proclaim this great mercy of Mine towards souls of sinners. Let the sinner not be afraid to approach Me. The flames of mercy are burning Me – clamoring to be spent; I want to pour them out upon these souls. (Diary,50)

The Lord said to me, **My daughter, do not tire of proclaiming My mercy. In this way you will refresh this Heart of Mine, which burns with a flame of pity for sinners. Tell My priests that hardened sinners will** repent on hearing their words when they speak about **My unfathomable mercy, about the compassion I have for them in My Heart. To priests who proclaim and extol My mercy, I will give wondrous power; I will anoint their words and touch the hearts of those to whom they will speak.** (Diary,1521)

The Chaplet of the Divine Mercy:

The words with which I entreated God are these: **Eternal Father, I offer You the Body and Blood, Soul and Divinity of Your dearly beloved son, Our Lord Jesus Christ for our sins and those of the whole world; for the sake of His sorrowful Passion, have mercy on us.** (Diary, 475)

The next morning, when I entered chapel, I heard these words interiorly: **Every time you enter the chapel, immediately recite the prayer which I taught you yesterday.** When I had said the prayer, in my soul I heard these words: **This prayer will serve to appease My wrath. You will recite it for nine days, on the beads of the rosary, in the following manner: First of all, you will say one OUR FATHER and HAIL MARY and** the I BELIEVE IN GOD. Then on the OUR FATHER beads you will say the following words: "Eternal Father, I offer You the Body and Blood, Soul and divinity of Your dearly beloved Son, Our Lord Jesus Christ, in atonement for our sins and those of the whole world." On the HAIL MARY beads you will say the following words: "For the sake of His sorrowful Passion have mercy on us and on the whole world." In conclusion, three times you will recite these words: "Holy God, Holy Mighty One, Holy Immortal One, have mercy on us and on the whole world." (Diary, 476)

Once, as I was going down the hall to the kitchen, I heard these words in my soul: **Say unceasingly the chaplet that I have taught you. Whoever will recite it will receive great mercy at the hour of death. Priests will recommend it to sinners as their last hope of salvation. Even if there were a sinner most hardened, if he were to recite this chaplet only once, he would receive grace from My infinite mercy. I desire that the whole world know My infinite mercy. I desire to grant unimaginable graces to those souls who trust in My mercy.** (Diary, 687)

The Lord's Promise: **The souls that say this chaplet will be embraced by My mercy during their lifetime and especially at the hour of their death.** (Diary, 754)

While I was saying the chaplet, I heard a voice which said, **Oh, what great graces I will grant to souls who say this chaplet; the very depths of My tender mercy are stirred for the sake of those who say the chaplet. Write down these words, My daughter. Speak to the world about My mercy; let all mankind recognize My unfathomable mercy. It is a sign for the end times; after it will come (230) the day of justice. While there is still time, let them have recourse to the fount of My mercy; let them profit from the Blood and Water which gushed forth for them.** (Diary,848)

Write this for the benefit of distressed souls; when a soul sees and realized the gravity of its sins, when the whole abyss of the misery into which it immersed itself is displayed before its eyes, let it not despair, but with trust let it throw itself into the arms of My mercy, as a child into the arms of its beloved mother. These souls (125) have a right of priority to My

compassionate Heart, they have first access to My mercy. Tell them that no soul that has called upon My mercy has been disappointed or brought to shame. I delight particularly in a soul which has placed its trust in My goodness." (Diary,1541)

Jesus, I trust in you

I promise that the soul that will venerate this image will not perish. I also promise victory over [its] enemies already here on earth, especially at the hour of death. I Myself will defend it as My own glory. (Diary,48)

My daughter, if I demand through you that people revere My mercy, you should be the first to distinguish yourself by this confidence in My mercy. I demand from you deeds of mercy, which are to arise out of love for Me. You are to show mercy to your neighbors always and everywhere. You must not shrink from this or try to excuse or absolve yourself from it. I am giving you three ways of exercising mercy toward your neighbor: the first- by deed, the second – by word, the third – by prayer. In these three degrees is contained the fullness of mercy, and it is an unquestionable proof of love for Me. By this means a soul glorifies and pays reverence to My mercy. Yes, the first Sunday after Easter is the Feast of Mercy, but there must also be acts of mercy, and I demand the worship of My mercy through the solemn celebration of the Feast and through the veneration of the image which is painted. By means of this image I shall grant many graces to souls. It is to be a reminded of the demands of My mercy, because even the strongest (163) faith is of no avail without works. (Diary,742)

During prayer I head these words within me: The two rays denote Blood and Water. The pale ray stands for the Water which makes souls righteous. The red ray stands for the Blood which is the life of souls……

These two rays issued forth from the very depths of My tender mercy when My agonized Heart was opened by a lance on the Cross. These rays shield souls from the wrath of My Father. Happy is the one who will dwell in their shelter, for the just hand of God shall not lay hold of him. I desire that the first Sunday after Easter be the Feast of Mercy. (Diary,299)

Jesus. – From all My wounds, like from streams, mercy flows for souls, but the wound in My Heart is the fountain of unfathomable mercy. From this fountain spring all graces for souls. The flames of compassion burn Me. I desire greatly to pour them out upon souls. Speak to the whole world about My mercy. (Diary,1190)

The Feast of Mercy:

My image already is in your soul. I desire that there be a Feast of Mercy. I want this image, which you will paint with a brush, to be solemnly blessed on the first Sunday after Easter; that Sunday is to be the Feast of Mercy. (Diary,49)

My daughter, tell the whole world about My inconceivable (138) mercy. I desire that the Feast of Mercy[139] be a refuge and shelter for all souls, and especially for poor sinners. On that day the very depths of My tender mercy are open. I pour out a whole ocean of graces upon those souls who approach the Fount of My Mercy. The soul that will go to Confession and receive Holy Communion shall obtain complete forgiveness of sins and punishment. On that day all the divine floodgates through which graces flow are opened. Let no soul fear to draw near to Me, even though its sins be as scarlet. My mercy is so great that no mind, be it of man or of angel, will be able to fathom it throughout all eternity. Everything that exists has come forth from the very depths of My most tender mercy. Every soul in its relation to Me will contemplate My love and mercy throughout eternity. The Feast of Mercy emerged from My very depths of tenderness. (139) It is My desire that it be solemnly celebrated on the first Sunday after Easter. Mankind will not have peace until it turns to the Fount of My Mercy. (Diary,699)

Say, My daughter, that the Feast of My Mercy has issued forth from My very depths for the consolation of the whole world. (Diary,1517)

At three o'clock:

At three o'clock, implore My mercy, especially for sinners; and, if only for a brief moment, immerse yourself in My Passion, particularly in My abandonment at the moment of agony. This is the hour of great mercy for the whole world. I will allow you to enter into My mortal sorrow. In this hour, I will refuse nothing to the soul that makes a request of me in virtue of My Passion....... (Diary, 1320)

I remind you, My daughter, that as often as you hear the clock strike the third hour, immerse yourself completely in My mercy, adoring and glorifying it; invoke its omnipotence for the whole world, and particularly for poor sinners; for at that moment mercy was opened wide for every (145) soul. In this hour you can obtain everything for yourself and for others for the asking; it was the hour of grace for the whole world – mercy triumphed over justice. (Diary, 1572)

MARY FAUSTINA KOWALSKA
1905-1938

Sister Mary Faustina, an apostle of the Divine Mercy, belongs today to the group of the most popular and well-known saints of the Church. Through her the Lord Jesus communicates to the world the great message of God's mercy and reveals the pattern of Christian perfection based on trust in God and on the attitude of mercy toward one's neighbors1905 – 1938 She was born on August 25, 1905 in G»ogowiec in Poland of a poor and religious family of peasants, the third of ten children. She was baptized with the name Helena in the parish Church ofÐwinice Warckie. From a very tender age she stood out because of her love of prayer, work, obedience, and also her sensitivity to the poor. At the age of nine she made her first Holy Communion living this moment very profoundly in her awareness of the presence of the Divine Guest within her soul. She attended school for three years. At the age of sixteen she left home and went to work as a housekeeper in Aleksandrów, °ódï and Ostrówek in order to find the means of supporting herself and of helping her parents.

At the age of seven she had already felt the first stirrings of a religious vocation. After finishing school, she wanted to enter the convent but her parents would not give her permission. Called during a vision of the Suffering Christ, on August 1, 1925 she entered the Congregation of the Sisters of Our Lady of Mercy and took the name Sister Mary Faustina. She lived in the Congregation for thirteen years and lived in several religious houses. She spent time at Kraków, P»ock and Vilnius, where she worked as a cook, gardener and porter.

Externally nothing revealed her rich mystical interior life. She zealously performed her tasks and faithfully observed the rule of religious life. She was recollected and at the same time very natural, serene and full of kindness and disinterested love for her neighbor. Although her life was apparently insignificant, monotonous and dull, she hid within herself an extraordinary union with God.

It is the mystery of the Mercy of God which

she contemplated in the word of God as well as in the everyday activities of her life that forms the basis of her spirituality. The process of contemplating and getting to know the mystery of God's mercy helped develop within Sr. Mary Faustina the attitude of child-like trust in God as well as mercy toward the neighbors. O my Jesus, each of Your saints reflects one of Your virtues; I desire to reflect Your compassionate heart, full of mercy; I want to glorify it. Let Your mercy, O Jesus, be impressed upon my heart and soul like a seal, and this will be my badge in this and the future life (Diary 1242). Sister Faustina was a faithful daughter of the Church which she loved like a Mother and a Mystic Body of Jesus Christ. Conscious of her role in the Church, she cooperated with God's mercy in the task of saving lost souls. At the specific request of and following the example of the Lord Jesus, she made a sacrifice of her own life for this very goal. In her spiritual life she also distinguished herself with a love of the Eucharist and a deep devotion to the Mother of Mercy.

The years she had spent at the convent were

filled with extraordinary gifts, such as: revelations, visions, hidden stigmata, participation in the Passion of the Lord, the gift of bilocation, the reading of human souls, the gift of prophecy, or the rare gift of mystical engagement and marriage. The living relationship with God, the Blessed Mother, the Angels, the Saints, the souls in Purgatory — with the entire supernatural world — was as equally real for her as was the world she perceived with her senses. In spite of being so richly endowed with extraordinary graces, Sr. Mary Faustina knew that they do not in fact constitute sanctity. In her Diary she wrote: Neither graces, nor revelations, nor raptures, nor gifts granted to a soul make it perfect, but rather the intimate union of the soul with God. These gifts are merely ornaments of the soul, but constitute neither its essence nor its perfection. My sanctity and perfection consist in the close union of my will with the will of God (Diary 1107).

The Lord Jesus chose Sr. Mary Faustina as the Apostle and "Secretary" of His Mercy, so that she could tell the world about His great message. In the Old

Covenant — He said to her —I sent prophets wielding thunderbolts to My people. Today I am sending you with My mercy to the people of the whole world. I do not want to punish aching mankind, but I desire to heal it, pressing it to My Merciful Heart (Diary 1588).

The mission of Sister Mary Faustina consists in 3 tasks:

– reminding the world of the truth of our faith revealed in the Holy Scripture about the merciful love of God toward every human being.

– Entreating God's mercy for the whole world and particularly for sinners, among others through the practice of new forms of devotion to the Divine Mercy presented by the Lord Jesus, such as: the veneration of the image of the Divine Mercy with the inscription: Jesus, I Trust in You, the feast of the Divine Mercy celebrated on the first Sunday after Easter, chaplet to the Divine Mercy and prayer at the Hour of Mercy (3 p.m.). The Lord Jesus attached great promises to the above forms of devotion, provided one entrusted one's life to God and practiced active love of one's neighbor.

– The third task in Sr. Mary Faustina's mission consists in initiating the apostolic movement of the Divine Mercy which undertakes the task of proclaiming and entreating God's mercy for the world and strives for Christian perfection, following the precepts laid down by the Blessed Sr. Mary Faustina. The precepts in question require the faithful to display an attitude of child-like trust in God which expresses itself in fulfilling His will, as well as in the attitude of mercy toward one's neighbors. Today, this movement within the Church involves millions of people throughout the world; it comprises religious congregations, lay institutes, religious, brotherhoods, associations, various communities of apostles of the Divine Mercy, as well as individual people who take up the tasks which the Lord Jesus communicated to them through Sr. Mary Faustina.

The mission of the Blessed Sr. Mary Faustina was recorded in her Diary which she kept at the specific request of the Lord Jesus and her confessors. In it, she recorded faithfully all of the Lord Jesus' wishes and also described the encounters between her soul and Him. Secretary of My most profound mystery — the Lord Jesus said to Sr. Faustina — know that your task is to write down everything that I make known to you about My mercy, for the benefit of those who by reading these things will be comforted in their souls and will have the courage to approach Me (Diary 1693). In an extraordinary way, Sr. Mary Faustina's work sheds light on the mystery of the Divine Mercy. It delights not only the simple and uneducated people, but also scholars who look upon it as an additional source of theo-logical research. The Diary has been translated into many languages, among others, English, German, Italian, Spanish, French, Portuguese, Arabic, Russian, Hungarian, Czech and Slovak.

Sister Mary Faustina, consumed by tuberculosis and by innumerable sufferings which she accepted as a voluntary sacrifice for sinners, died in Krakow at the age of just thirty three on October 5, 1938 with a reputation for spiritual maturity and a mystical union with God. The reputation of the holiness of her life grew as did the cult to the Divine Mercy and the graces she obtained from God through her intercession. In the years 1965-67, the investigative Process into her life and heroic virtues was undertaken in Krakow and in the year 1968, the Beatification Process was initiated in Rome. The latter came to an end in December 1992. On April 18, 1993 our Holy Father John Paul II raised Sister Faustina to the glory of the altars. Sr. Mary Faustina's remains rest at the Sanctuary of the Divine Mercy in Krakow.

THE CANONIZATION OF SR MARY FAUSTINA KOWALSKA, happened on Saint Peter's square on Sunday, 30 April 2000

THE CHAPLET OF THE DIVINE MERCY

Make the Sign of the Cross

In the name of the Father, and of the Son, and of the Holy Spirit. Amen.

Opening Prayers

You expired, Jesus, but the source of life gushed forth for souls, and the ocean of mercy opened up for the whole world. O Fount of Life, unfathomable Divine Mercy, envelop the whole world and empty Yourself out upon us.

(Repeat three times)

O Blood and Water, which gushed forth from the Heart of Jesus as a fountain of Mercy for us, I trust in You!

Our Father

Our Father, Who art in heaven, hallowed be Thy name; Thy kingdom come; Thy will be done on earth as it is in heaven. Give us this day our daily bread; and forgive us our trespasses as we forgive those who trespass against us; and lead us not into temptation, but deliver us from evil, Amen.

Hail Mary

Hail Mary, full of grace. The Lord is with thee. Blessed art thou amongst women, and blessed is the fruit of thy womb, Jesus. Holy Mary, Mother of God, pray for us sinners, now and at the hour of our death, Amen.

The Apostle's Creed

I believe in God, the Father almighty, Creator of heaven and earth, and in Jesus Christ, His only Son, our Lord, who was conceived by the Holy Spirit, born of the Virgin Mary, suffered under Pontius Pilate, was crucified, died and was buried; He descended into hell; on the third day He rose again from the dead; He ascended into heaven, and is seated at the right hand of God the Father almighty; from there He will come to judge the living and the dead. I believe in the Holy Spirit, the holy catholic Church, the communion of saints, the forgiveness of sins, the resurrection of the body, and life everlasting. Amen.

The Eternal Father

Eternal Father, I offer you the Body and Blood, Soul and Divinity of Your Dearly Beloved Son, Our Lord, Jesus Christ, in atonement for our sins and those of the whole world.

On the Ten Small Beads of Each Decade

For the sake of His sorrowful Passion, have mercy on us and on the whole world.

Repeat for the remaining decades

Saying the "Eternal Father" on the "Our Father" bead and then 10 "For the sake of His sorrowful Passion" on the following "Hail Mary" beads.

Conclude with Holy God

(Repeat three times)

Holy God, Holy Mighty One, Holy Immortal One, have mercy on us and on the whole world.

Optional Closing Prayer

Eternal God, in whom mercy is endless and the treasury of compassion — inexhaustible, look kindly upon us and increase Your mercy in us, that in difficult moments we might not despair nor become despondent, but with great confidence submit ourselves to Your holy will, which is Love and Mercy itself.

DANIEL G. BRAVO

www.ingramcontent.com/pod-product-compliance
Lightning Source LLC
Chambersburg PA
CBHW051844040426
42447CB00006B/693